Learning Tree
1 2 3

Words at Work

By Deborah Manley
Illustrated by Joanne Flindall

CHERRYTREE BOOKS

Read this book and see if you can answer the questions.
Ask an adult or an older friend to tell you if your answers
are right or to help you if you find the questions difficult.
Often there is more than one answer to a question.

A Cherrytree Book

Designed and produced by
A S Publishing

First published 1991
by Cherrytree Press Ltd
a subsidiary of
The Chivers Company Ltd
Windsor Bridge Road
Bath, Avon BA2 3AX

Copyright © Cherrytree Press Ltd 1991

British Library Cataloguing in Publication Data
Manley, Deborah
  Words at work.
  1. English language. Words (Vocabulary)
  I. Title   II. Flindall, Joanne   III. Series
  428.1

  ISBN 0-7451-5150-7

Printed and bound in Italy by L.E.G.O. s.p.a., Vicenza

What do you see here?

3

What do you see here?

Can you name the things you see?

What words did you use for the things in the classroom?

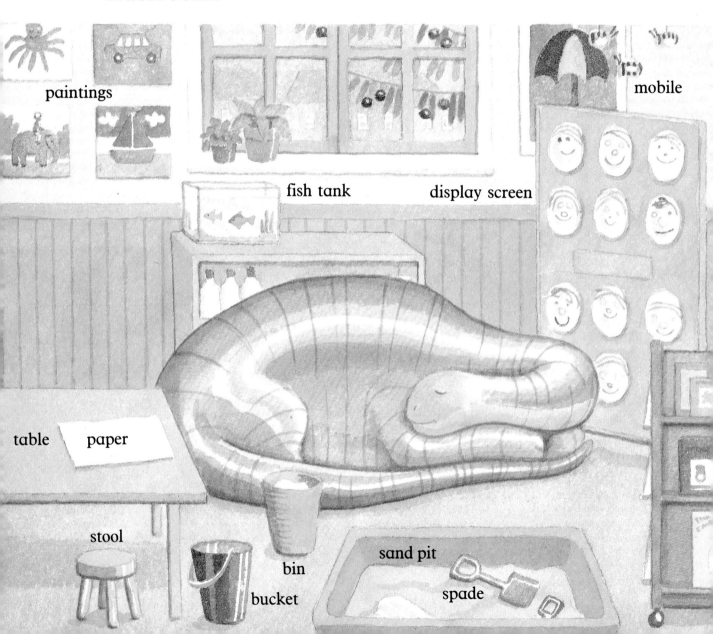

paintings

mobile

fish tank

display screen

table

paper

stool

bin

bucket

sand pit

spade

Did you use these words? Did you use others?
Did you see a dinosaur?

crayons

windows

plant

flowers

easel

ladder

cupboard

chair

bookcase

jug

bottle

broom

water table

mat

boat

There are different kinds of words.
They have different jobs to do.

Some words name people, places or things.
They are called nouns. These words are all nouns.

staff room

notice board

door

teacher

tail

chair

waste-paper basket

Think of nouns for these people.

Think of nouns for these places.

Think of nouns for these things.

What is happening here?
What are the children doing?

12

What is the dinosaur doing?
What is the teacher doing?

13

Doing words are called verbs.
They tell us what everyone is doing.
These words are all verbs.

Who is doing these things?
skipping, flying, climbing, fighting, eating.

Which of these words are nouns?

girl
boy
spoon
eat
drink
fork
glass
table
look
knife
soup
spill

Which of these words are verbs?

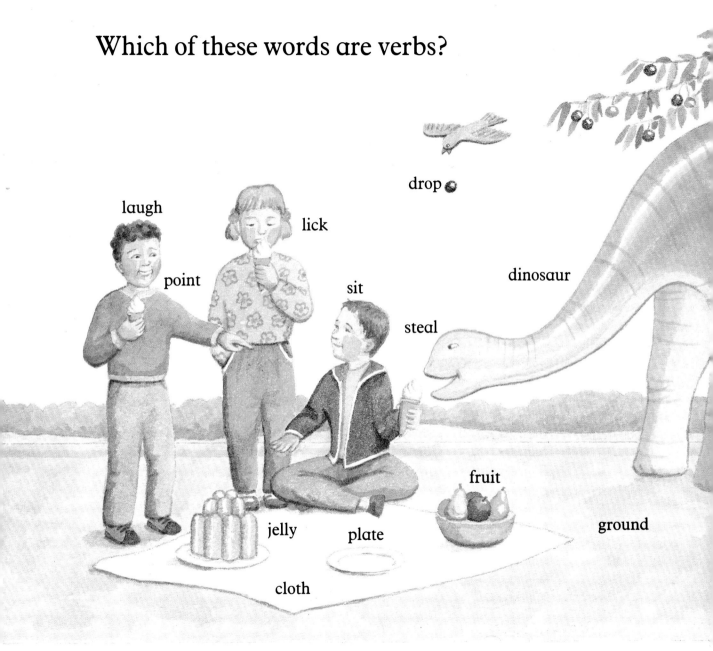

drop

laugh

lick

point

sit

steal

dinosaur

fruit

jelly

plate

ground

cloth

You use nouns and verbs together in sentences.

The teacher is looking for the chalk.
Sue passes a note to Leo.

This girl is doing her work.
Who is cheating?

More about words

Nouns name things. Verbs are action words. There are other kinds of words too. They have different jobs.

Adjectives
Some words tell you more about nouns. They describe people, places or things. How would you describe these dinosaurs? One is big and one is small. Big and small are adjectives. They describe the dinosaurs. Think of some adjectives to describe yourself and your friends.

Adverbs
Some words tell you more about verbs. They describe how something is being done. One dinosaur is running fast. The other dinosaur is running slowly. Fast and slowly are adverbs. Which word in this sentence is an adverb? The dinosaur eats daintily.

What kind of word?
There are lots of other kinds of words that we use all the time. It is hard to get to know about them all at once. Don't worry if you don't know what kind of a word you are reading.

Tenses
Verbs change to show us when something happened.
   The dinosaur sleeps.
   The dinosaur is sleeping.
   The dinosaur slept.
   The dinosaur was sleeping.
   The dinosaur will sleep.

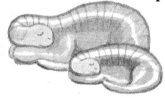

More things to do

Sorting nouns and verbs
Collect words that you like or find useful. Keep nouns in one list and verbs in another. Keep a third list for other kinds of words. Sort your nouns into separate lists of people, places and things. Your lists will help you with the next game.

Person, place or thing?
Play this game with a friend or friends. One person calls out a noun. The others say whether it is a person, place or thing.

Who does what?
Cut up 20 pieces of card. On 10 of them write the name of an animal. On the other 10 write different things that animals do. You might start with these cards:

gorilla	walks
fish	eats
snake	sleeps
bee	scratches

Each person takes a noun and a verb card. Then they pretend to be the animal performing the action. Have you ever seen a fish scratching?

Shh! its a verb!
Someone reads slowly from a book. Everyone else listens. Whenever the reader reads out a noun, everyone claps their hands once. Whenever the reader reads out a verb, the listeners stay very quiet. Everyone puts a finger over their lips. You are out if you do the wrong thing at the wrong time.

Words from word
Think of a long word like elephant. See how many short words you can make from it. Here are some: ant, peel, hen, eel. When you can think of no more, sort your words out. Some will be nouns, some will be verbs. Some like peel will be both! And others will be neither.

1

1 What do we call words that name a person, place or thing?

2 What do we call 'doing' words?

3 Is the word cat a noun or a verb?

4 Draw pictures of people doing these things:
dancing waving sitting

5 Use nouns and verbs to say what is happening in the picture.

2

6 Draw pictures of these people:
teacher father clown

7 Draw pictures of these places:
school house circus

8 Draw pictures of these things:
book bed ball

9 What is a noun?

10 Are these words all nouns?
teacher school book

11 Which of these words are nouns?
tree leaf twig grows

12 What is a verb?

13 Which of these words are verbs?
shout sing whisper mouth

14 Which is the verb in this sentence?
The naughty dog chases the cat.

3

15 Keep a notebook for your words. Put the answers to the questions in this book in your notebook. Write down any questions you want to ask about words. Write down words that you don't know. You can look them up in a dictionary later.

16 The word hand is a noun. Your hand has parts. Your thumb is one part. Can you name the others?

17 Which of these two words is an adjective? naughty dog

18 Which of these two words is an adverb? walked slowly

19 Find a paragraph (a group of sentences) in an old newspaper. Colour the nouns green and the verbs red. Leave the other words. Are there more nouns or more verbs?

20 Lots of words can be nouns or verbs. Do you know two meanings for each of these words? break drive watch jump switch train paint. If you don't know them, look in a dictionary. In dictionaries nouns are usually marked n. and verbs are marked v.

21 What other words do you know that can be nouns or verbs?

22 We call our names and the names of places proper nouns. We give them capital letters to start with like this: Terry, Miss Black, Edinburgh. What proper nouns do you know? Make a list of your friends' names.

23 What are you doing at the moment? Write down verbs for what you and others around you are doing. Write down nouns for what you and your friends are wearing. Think of some adjectives to describe your friends!

Index